Copyright © 2013 by Ruby Roth. All rights reserved. No portion of this book, except for brief review, may be reproduced, stored in a retrieval system, or transmitted in any form or by any means—electronic, mechanical, photocopying, recording, or otherwise—without the written permission of the publisher. For information contact North Atlantic Books.

Published by
North Atlantic Books
Berkeley, California

All artwork by Ruby Roth
Cover and book design by Ruby Roth
Printed in the United States of America

V Is for Vegan: The ABCs of Being Kind is sponsored and published by the Society for the Study of Native Arts and Sciences (dba North Atlantic Books), an educational nonprofit based in Berkeley, California, that collaborates with partners to develop cross-cultural perspectives, nurture holistic views of art, science, the humanities, and healing, and seed personal and global transformation by publishing work on the relationship of body, spirit, and nature.

North Atlantic Books' publications are available through most bookstores.
For further information, visit our website at www.northatlanticbooks.com or call 800-733-3000.

Library of Congress Cataloging-in-Publication Data

Roth, Ruby.
 V is for vegan : the ABCs of being kind / written and illustrated by
Ruby Roth.
     pages cm
 Audience: Age 3-7.
 Summary: "Introducing three-to-five-year-olds to the "ABCs" of a vegan lifestyle, V Is for Vegan is a must-have for vegan and vegetarian parents! Acclaimed author and artist Ruby Roth (That's Why We Don't Eat Animals, Vegan Is Love) brings her characteristic insight, compassion, and good humor to a younger audience, presenting the often-controversial and challenging subjects of animal rights and the vegan diet in an easy-to-understand and teachable format. Roth introduces little herbivores to the major vegan food groups (beans, grains, nuts, vegetables, and fruits) as well as the ways we can protect animals and the environment. Colorful, upbeat, and fun, V Is for Vegan helps boost the confidence of vegan children about to enter school and helps parents explain their ethical worldview in a way their young children will grasp." -- Provided by publisher.
 ISBN 978-1-58394-649-7 (hardback)
 1. Veganism--Juvenile literature. 2. Animal welfare--Juvenile
literature. 3. Alphabet books. I. Title.
 TX392.R743 2013
 613.2'622--dc23
                         2013008253

Printed on recycled paper

Printed and bound by Qualibre/CGPrinting, January 2016, In the United States.
Job# 113.
3 4 5 6 7 8 9 Qualibre/CG Printing 20 19 18 17 16

V Is for Vegan

The ABCs of Being Kind

Written and Illustrated
by Ruby Roth

North Atlantic Books
Berkeley, California

Aa

is for animals—
friends, not food.
We don't eat our friends,
they'd find it quite rude.

Bb is for beauty,
enjoy it together.

Cc is for clothing, no skins, fur, or feathers.

Dd is for dairy.
Moo! Milk is for cows.

Ee is for eggs—
from a chicken's butt?!
Wow.

Ff is for fruit, fresh, dried, or in jelly.

grapes

raisins

grape jam

jelly

Gg is for grains, go get in my belly!

rice   quinoa   corn   millet

rye   barley   oats   wheat

Hh

is for honey?
That's food for bees!
Bees need their honey
when temperatures freeze.

Ii is for insects, not happy in jars.

Jj is for jail,
like zoos and their bars.

L l is for legumes, often called beans.

garbanzo
bean

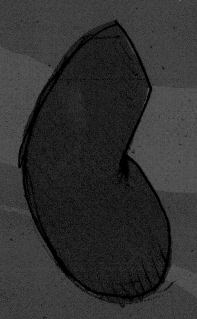

kidney
bean

lentil

black-eyed
pea

black
bean

human
bean

Mm is for meat,
from coconuts, of course!

Nn is for nuts, a fine energy source.

Oo is for oils
to grow, bend, and dance.

Avocado   Coconut Oil   Flax Oil   Olive Oil   Hemp seed oil   Olives

Good oils give us energy and help our brains, hearts, and joints.

Pp is for protein.

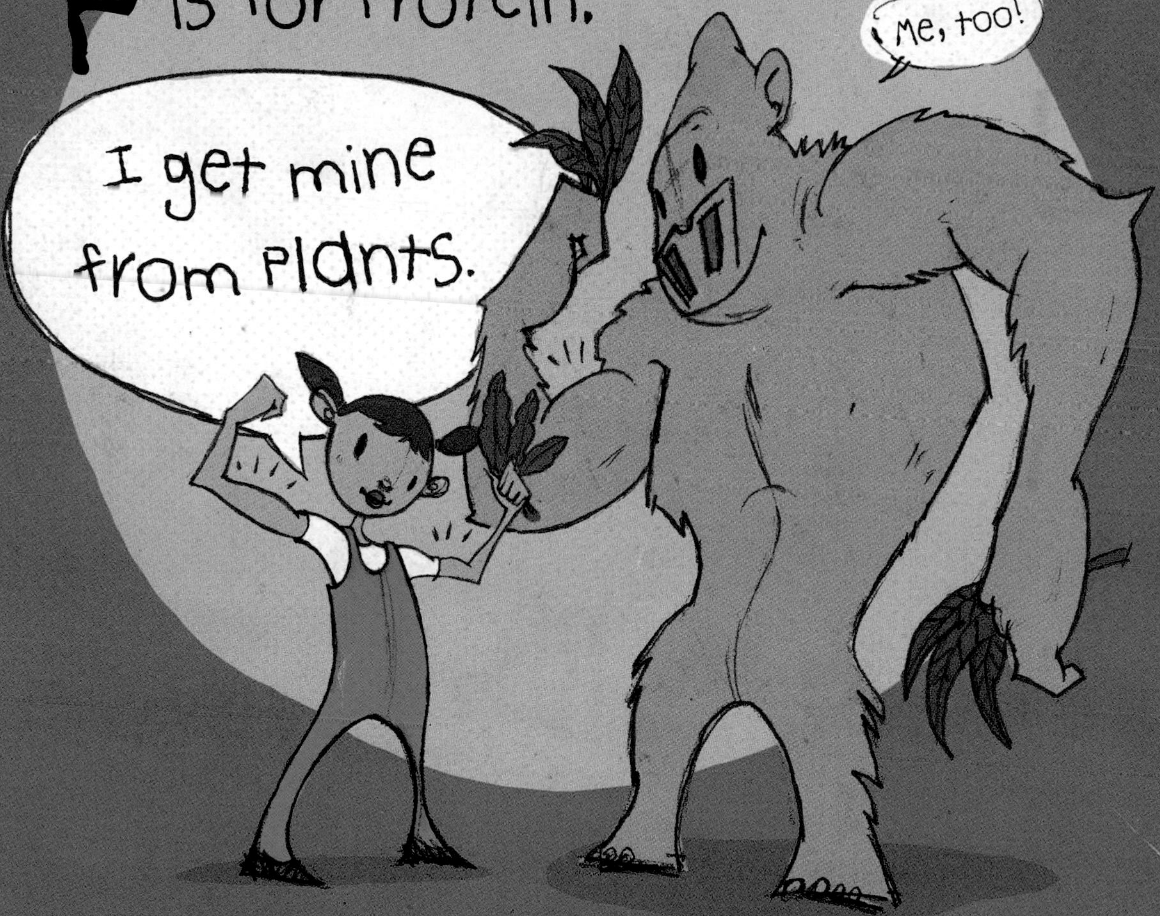

Protein helps our muscles grow!

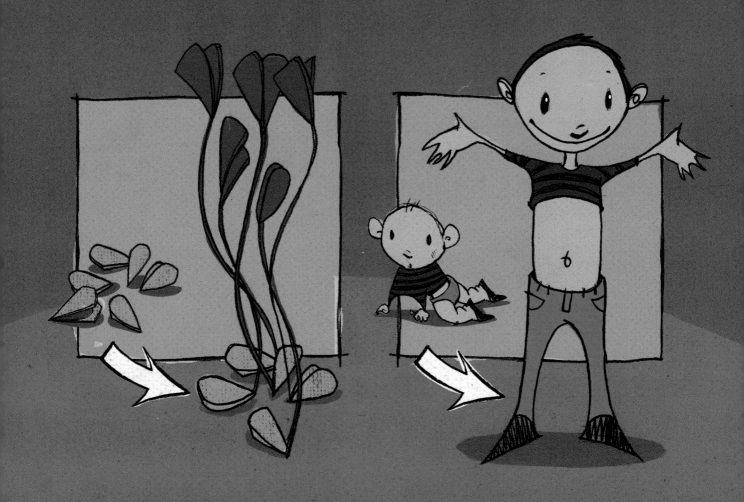

Ss is for seeds.
Just like you, they sprout, too.

Tt to treat others as they should treat you.

No testing on animals!

Uu is for use and re-use.

Please don't waste!

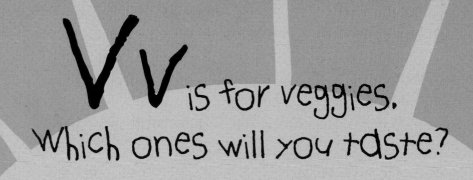

Vv is for veggies.
Which ones will you taste?

Ww is for world,
it glows blue and green.
We only have one,
so please keep it clean.

X x marks the spot
for the seeds that we scatter.

Zz is for zero,
no animals harmed.
Hooray for the day
when they're no longer farmed!

We've come to the end,
but it's just the start!
There are many more
ways to have heart—
do your part.

This book uses Endeavour recycled paper.
For every 4,000 copies of this book
printed, we have saved:

- 4 trees
- 12 pounds of waterborn waste
- 1,766 gallons of wastewater flow
- 195 pounds of solid waste
- 385 pounds net greenhouse gases
- 2,945,250 BTUs of energy

30% PCW

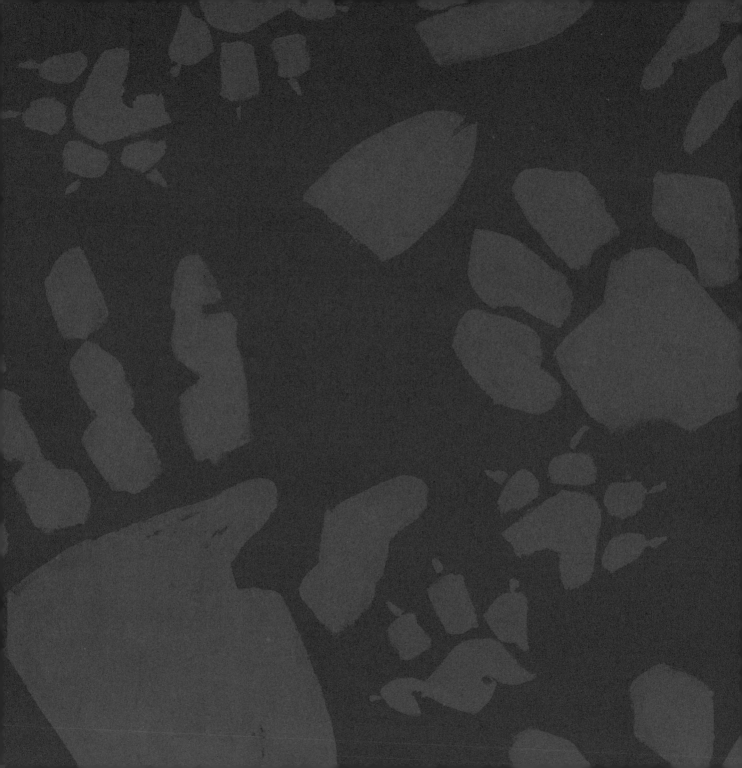